Orthodox Icon Patterns Vol II Revised

———

Patterns & Sketches for Iconographers

by **RB Cass**

ISBN- 9798622803475

Edited by Mother Lyudmila Formatted by Keilah Cass

TABLE OF CONTENTS

1	Nativity
3	Christ Emmanuel
5	Pantocrator
7	Theotokos Virgin of Antioch
9	Archangel Michael
11	Holy Martyr Agrippina of Rome
13	Saint Aidan
15	Saint Andrew
17	Saint Apollonia
19	Saint Argyre
21	Holy Martyr Cecilia
23	Saint Columba
25	Saint David of Thessalonica
27	Saint Dwynwen
29	Saint Ephraim of Nea Makri
31	Holy Great Martyr Euphemia
33	Saint Frideswide
35	Saint George the Great Martyr
37	Saint Hermione
39	Saint Ita of Abbess of Killeedy
41	Saint Juliana
43	Saint Killian
45	Saint Lydia
47	Saint Mamas of Caesarea (1)
49	Saint Mamas of Caesarea (2)
51	Saint Nicholas
53	Righteous Noah
55	Saint Oda of Brabant
57	Saint Paul of Thebes
59	Saint Sampson the Hospitable
61	Saint Spyridon the Wonderworker
63	Saint Stylianos (Stylian)
65	Holy Martyrs Timothy & Maura
67	Saint Xenia of Kalamata
69	Anzer Cross

71	Fabric — Background Patterns
73	Fabric — Antiocha
74	Fabric — Floral Wall
75	Fabric — Juliana
76	Fabric or Background — Starburst
77	Fabric — Pods
78	Background — Poppy
79	Fabric — Palm (1)
80	Fabric — Palm (2)
81	Background — Trellis
83	Borders
85	Border — Angel (Ethiopian Style)
86	Border — Ropely (Ethiopian Style)
87	Border — Star (Ethiopian Style)
88	Border — Trellis
89	Border — Simple
91	Halos
93	Halo — Emmanuel
94	Halo — Lothea
95	Halo — Polytas
96	Halo — Flowers
97	Halo — Saint Nicholas
98	Halo — Salina
99	Lettering
101	Script — Almaznyye
102	Script —Danica (Morning Star)
103	Script — Evgenia
104	Script — Theodore
105	A Prayer on New Icons That Are Donated to the Church
106	The Blessing of Icons
107	Order for the Blessing & Sanctification of Icons
109	A Prayer for Consecrating an Iconographer
110	Iconographer's Prayer
111	Index — Date of Commemoration
112	Index — Name of Saint
113	About the Author

Nativity
(Ethiopian)

Ephraim the Syrian on Christ's Divine and Human Natures
If he was not flesh, why was Mary introduced at all? — And if he was not God, whom was Gabriel calling Lord? If he was not flesh, who was lying in the manger? — And if he was not God, whom did the Angels come down and glorify? If he was not flesh, who was wrapped in swaddling clothes? — And if he was not God, whom did the shepherds worship? — If he was not flesh, whom did Joseph circumcise? — And if he was not God, in whose honour did the star speed through the heavens? — If he was not flesh, whom did Mary suckle? — And if he was not God, to whom did the Magi offer gifts? — If he was not flesh, whom did Symeon carry in his arms? — And if he was not God, to whom did he say, "Let me depart in peace"?

....

COLOURS

Swaddling cloth – Cream shades with Celadon Design
Blanket – Deep Yellow and Gold Oxide
Design on blanket – Norwegian Orange
Theotokos under Robe – Indian Red Oxide with Red Earth
Sleeve – Indian Red Oxide with Red Earth
Theotokos head cover & over robe – Celadon in various shades
Theotokos Cuff – Yellow Oxide
Joseph under robe – Green Oxide
Joseph over robe – Red Earth
Under Saddle Cloths – Naphthol Red Light
Upper Saddle Cloth – Cream with Red designs
Camels – Gold Oxide and Raw Sienna
Camel bridles – Brown Earth
Angel under robe – Green Oxide
Angel outer robe – Norwegian Orange with a touch of Napthol Red Light
Angel Wings – Green Oxide and Gold Oxide

Christ Emmanuel

Matthew 1:23 King James (KJV)

Behold, a virgin shall be with child, and shall bring forth a son, and they shall call his name Emmanuel, which being interpreted is, God with us.

Isaiah 7:14 King James (KJV)

Therefore the Lord himself shall give you a sign; Behold, a virgin shall conceive, and bear a son, and shall call his name Immanuel.

1 Timothy 3:16 King James (KJV)

And without controversy great is the mystery of godliness: God was manifest in the flesh, justified in the Spirit, seen of angels, preached unto the Gentiles, believed on in the world, received up into glory.

. . . .

COLOURS

Background – Storm Blue
Cloak – Red Ochre
Band over waist – Red Ochre
Under Robe – Gold Ochre

ĪС ХС

Ѡ Н

ЄMMA ~NЦЄЛ

4

Pantocrator
(Almighty, All-powerful or Ruler of All)

———

On the halo of Christ in inscribed the letters O Ω N – 'He Who Is'.

Revelation 1:8 – Irmos of Ode V

I am Alpha and Omega, the beginning and the ending, saith the Lord, which is, and which was and which is to come, the Almighty.

John 1:14 – Irmos of Ode V

And the Word was made flesh, and dwelt among us, and we beheld his glory, the glory as of the only begotten of the Father, full of grace and truth.

Canon of Preparation for Holy Communion – Irmos of Ode V

O Lord, Giver of light and Creator of the ages, guide us in the light of Thy commandments, for we know none other God beside Thee.

....

COLOURS

Cloak – Deep Blue with touch of green
Robe – Deep Red with touch of Purple
Gospel outer page edges – Napthol Red Light
Gospel Cover – Gold Oxide with Gems and gold touches

Theotokos Virgin of Antioch
(Antiochitissa)

————

This pattern is based on the beautiful 15th century icon of Cyprus (Antiochitissa) and is so very loving, tender and sweet.

Beginners perhaps would like to paint the robe of the Theotokos without a decorative pattern, thereby making it quite a simple task but still very beautiful. Iconographers with experience will probably enjoy the detail work of the decoration on the robe.

Ode VII – Supplicatory Canon to the Most Holy Theotokos

For weakness of body and sickness of soul, O Theotokos, do thou vouch safe healing to those who with love draw near to thy protection, O Virgin, who for us gavest birth to Christ the Savior.

Ode IX – Supplicatory Canon to the Most Holy Theotokos

Fill my heart with joy, O Virgin, thou who didst receive the fullness of joy, and didst banish the grief of sin. O most holy Theotokos, save us.

....

COLOURS

Theotokos Robe – Indian Red Oxide with Gold fabric design
Christ Child Robe – Warm White with Yellow Grey low lights
Christ Child Blanket – Gold Oxide with Gold high lights

МР ΘΥ

ΑΝΤΙΟΧΙΤΙССΑ

ΙС ΧС

W

8

Archangel Michael
(Synaxis)

Commemorated — November 8

———————

The Holy Archangel Michael as a protector of soldiers, for victory over adversaries, a protector of aviation and as a proctor at the end of one's life.

Ekos III – Akathist to the Holy Archangel Michael
Rejoice, O Michael, great supreme commander, with all the hosts of Heaven!

Kontakion IV – Akathist to the Holy Archangel Michael
From the tempest of temptations and dangers do thou deliver us who with love and joy celebrate thy most radiant festival, O foremost of the angels; for thou art a great helper in misfortunes, and at the hour of death a guardian and intercessor against evil spirits for all that cry to thy and our Master and God: Alleluia!

....

COLOURS

Wings – Gold Oxide - Brown and Moss Green
Cloak – Rusty Red
Mail Armor – Nimbus Grey
Skirt under Armor – Antique Green
Shoes and leg bindings – Gold Oxide
Sleeve ends – Antique Green
Sword – Nimbus Grey
Sword Sheath – Red with Gold trim

10

Holy Martyr Agrippina of Rome

Circa +257
Commemorated — June 23

———

Saint Agrippina is a patron saint against evil spirits, leprosy, thunderstorms, sea storms, bacteria diseases and bacterial infections.

Hymn of Praise – by St. Nikolai Velimirovich

Agrippina, purer than the lily,
Of God's Son, the betrothed,
Her soul, brighter than a flame
And her faith, firmer than a rock.
To the Lord she prayed, while being flogged,
Chanted psalms while enduring the wounds,
Forgiving everyone and blessing all,
To God, Agrippina gave her spirit, the soul departed, the body remained.
The holy relics of St. Agrippina are the defense of the land of Sicily,
Medicine to the unfortunate and to the sick, and a protection from the evils.
By the prayers of Saint Agrippina
May many miseries pass us by.

....

COLOURS

Hood and cloak – Alizarine Crimson and Napthol Red
Under garment – Indigo
Neck band – Gold Oxide with Gold detail and Pearls
Palm Leaf – Pine Green
Cross – Gold

Saint Aidan

Bishop of Lindisfarne, Enlightener of Northumbria

Circa +651 AD
Commemorated — August 31

————

Aposticha of the Deposition; and Glory...

The islands of the sea leap for joy at thy memory, O Aidan, for on the Isle of Scattery, in the Ireland of thy birth, thou didst first undertake the monastic life with the venerable Senan, on the blessed Island of Iona in the land of the Picts didst attain spiritual maturity under Segenius, and didst found thine own monastery on the Holy Isle of Lindisfarne on the coast of Northumbria. Wherefore, in thee were the words of Isaiah the Prophet fulfilled, for thy sake was the glory of the Lord revealed in the isles of the sea, and the name of the Lord made glorious therein.

Vespers – Composed by Reader Isaac Lambertson

With the right-believing Kings Oswald and Oswin thou didst plant the Faith of Christ among the English, as a true apostle and disciple of the Saviour, O holy Aidan; and caring for orphans and children as a solicitous father, thou didst instill in them true piety and the knowledge of God; and with coins entrusted to thee in Christian charity thou didst purchase the freedom of many who languished in bitter thralldom and captivity. O holy hierarch, look down from heaven upon us, thy sinful children: by thine example teach us the virtues and lead us to the vision of God, and by thy supplications ransom us, the wretched, from slavery to death and the devil.

· ·

COLOURS

Stole – Cream shades
Crosses – Red with gold detail
Vestment – Indian Red Oxide with highlights
Sleeve – Olive Green
Cuff – Pearls and gold detail
Gospel – Red and Gold with various coloured gems

SAINT AIDAN

OF LINDIS FARNE

Saint Andrew

Archbishop of Crete

Circa 660 – 740 AD
Commemorated — July 4

————

Extracts from the Great Canon of Saint Andrew on Wednesday of the First Week of Lent:

Song 1: Extracts from the Great Canon of Saint Andrew, on Wednesday of the First Week of Lent
Eirmos: He is my Helper and Protector, and has become my salvation. This is my God and I will glorify Him, My father's God and I will exalt Him. For gloriously has He been glorified.
Refrain: Have mercy on me, O God, have mercy on me.

Song 5: Extracts from the Great Canon of Saint Andrew, on Wednesday of the First Week of Lent
Eirmos: Out of the night watching early for Thee, enlighten me, I pray, O Lover of men, and guide even me in Thy commandments, and teach me, O Saviour, to do Thy will.
Refrain: Have mercy on me, O God, have mercy on me.

Song 6: Extracts from the Great Canon of Saint Andrew, on Wednesday of the First Week of Lent
Eirmos: I cried with my whole heart to the merciful God, and He heard me from the lowest hell and raised my life out of corruption.
Refrain: Have mercy on me, O God, have mercy on me.

....

COLOURS

Stole – Green with Golden Yellow Crosses
Vestment – Gold Oxide with Gold and Blue design
Gospel Book – Napthol Red Light with gold highlights and Gems

16

Saint Apollonia

Circa 249 AD
Commemorated — February 9

Ecclesiastical history of Eusebius Pamphilus: Bishop of Caesarea, in Palestine, quoting a letter from Saint Dionysius of Alexandria

They also seized that admirable virgin Apollonia and beating her jaws, they broke out all her teeth, and kindling a fire before the city, threatened to burn her alive, unless she would repeat their impious expressions. She appeared at first to shrink a little, but when pressed to go, she suddenly sprang into the fire and was consumed.

. . . .

COLOURS

Background A – Stormblue, Blue Storm or Phthalo Blue very dark
Outline of Arch. E – Yellow Oxide/Iron Oxide Yellow (more sandy)
Florets B – Gold Leaf
Top Corner Flower and Leaves C – Gold Leaf
Top Corner border D – Indian Red Oxide
Head Cover – Rich Cream
Garment – Alizarine Dark or English Red Deep
Cross – Gold
Lettering – Red
Tools – Dark Brown
Teeth – White

SAINT APOLLONIA

18

Saint Argyre

(Argyra or Argyria)

Circa + April 5, 1721
Commemorated — April 30

Saint Argre is the patron saint of marriage and youth.

Troparion – in Tone IV

Thou didst put tyrants to shame through your tortures, O modest one, being shown forth, O much-suffering one, as strong as a diamond, O glorious martyr of Christ, thou showed forth in struggles love and zeal and unquenchable longing for Christ, the Saviour: wherefore, O Argyre, did He worthily glorify thee.

Aposticha

O all-glorious Argyre, you were just joined in marriage, as the pride of Prousa and the boast of Byzantium, when the prideful serpent, through the terrible tyrant tried to convince you to soil the virginity of your marriage. But you conquered him, ascending to the heavens with glory, where you now entreat the Risen God, to preserve the multitudes of the Orthodox in peace, and for us who in faith honour your grace-flowing body, grant forgiveness and great mercy.

....

COLOURS

Garment – Salmon Pink
Crowns – White with touches of Gold
Cross – Gold

SAINT ARGYRE

20

Holy Martyr Cecilia

3rd Century
Commemorated — November 22

————

Hymn of Praise: The Holy Martyr Cecilia – by St. Nikolai Velimirovich

Cecilia, strong in faith, rich in faith;
her faith is more beautiful than the stars,
more precious than gold.
She nailed herself to the Lord, as to the Cross,
and sacrificed youth, joy, marriage and honour for Christ!
The cruel demon could steal nothing from her;
and when only her body remained, she gave it to Christ.
For the love of Christ, she gave the whole world,
even two worlds: her body and her pure soul.
Thus does the flame of faith burn, and the flame of love,
and by that flame Cecilia glorified herself.

....

COLOURS

Head Cover – White with a light touch of Blue
Robe – Vermillion mixed with Pale Ochre
Flowers on Robe & Head cover – Pale Blue – Cobalt Blue Hue / Sapphire

SAINT CECILIA

Saint Columba

Circa 521 – 597 AD
Commemorated — June 6

————

Saint Columba's Prayer

O Lord, grant us that love which can never die, which will enkindle our lamps but not extinguish them, so that they may shine in us and bring light to others. Most dear Saviour, enkindle our lamps that they may shine forever in Thy temple. May we receive unquenchable light from Thee so that our darkness will be illuminated and the darkness of the world will be made less. Amen.

Troparion – Tone 5

By your God-inspired life you embodied both the mission and the dispersion of the Church, most glorious Father Columba. Using your repentance and voluntary exile, Christ our God raised you up as a beacon of the True Faith, an apostle to the heathen and an indicator of the Way of salvation. Wherefore O holy one, cease not to intercede for us that our souls may be saved.

....

COLOURS

Background – Mixed or Gold
Hood – Deep Blue touch of Black
Cloak – Indian Red, touch of Burnt sienna
Cross – Grey with white highlights
Under Garment – Light Apricot / Cream
Cuff – Light Apricot / Cream
Staff Head – Gold Leaf
Staff Pole – Wood Colour
Gospel Pages – Napthol Red Light
Gospel Cover – Red & Gold with gems

saint

columba

of

iona

24

Saint David of Thessalonica
The Dendrite

Circa 540 AD
Commemorated — June 26

———

Saint David received from God the gift of wonderworking, many people seeking his prayers were healed of various illnesses, as well as those who were possessed. He also gave spiritual counsel and comfort to all who came to him.

Kontakion – in Tone II

An Angel on earth, and stranger to all earthly things, thou madest a tree thy dwelling like an eagle's nest, whence, O David, thou didst soar up to Heaven, where thou didst find that Tree which in Eden we lost of old. Remember us all, who keep thy memory.

....

COLOURS

Cloak – Venetian Red
Under Riassa – Limonite
Leaves – Olive Green and light Bohemian Green

Saint Dwynwen

of Llanddwyn Island, Wales

Circa +460
Commemorated — January 25

_____

'Dwynwen' means 'she who leads a blessed life'

Saint Dwynwen is the patron of love and marriage, men and women pray for her intercession, that they may be granted a blessed, happy and successful marriage.

Saint Dwynwen helps not only those in love, but also the sick and those in need. Farmers in Wales consider her to be the patron of their animals. Countless cases of healing from various ailments were recorded and miracles continue to occur up to this day.

Holy Mother Dwynwen, pray to God for us!

....

COLOURS

Cloak and Hood – Terre Verte
Lining of Cloak – Deep Blue
Garment – Raw Sienna or Deep Ochre
Line around Bodice & down the front – Venetian Red
Cross – Gold or Deep Grey
Church – Stone grey
Hair – Burnt Sienna with shades

saint

dwyn wen

of

lland dwyn

Saint Ephraim of Nea Makri

Circa 1384 – 1426
Commemerated — May 5

God granted Saint Ephraim the ability to heal and even today there is a flow of reports of healings and answered prayer. He has delivered young people of addiction (drugs and alcohol and other addictions), protection against suicide, and restored faith to those who have lost all faith. Parents have been blessed after asking the saint for help for their children. All in all, Saint Ephraim has and is healing many different diseases, and is reported to be quick to answer the prayers of those who call upon him.

Kontakion

You dawned like a newly-revealed star through the revelation of your holy Relics, O Father, and you shine upon all with the rays of wonders, but ever fulfill the entreaties of those who faithfully hasten to you, O Saint Ephraim, and cry to you: Rejoice, O blessed Father.

Kontakion

Dissolving every confusion & bestowing joy, you appeared to the chase Abbess, and you revealed to her truly where your holy bones would be found. She, beholding this occurrence through God's revelation cried out: Alleluia

COLOURS

Cloak and Hat (Skufia) – Black with varying shades of blue highlights
Schema – Blue with Bright Red Cross
Under Garment – Hermatite or Brown Ochre
Light – Blue and grey
Belt – Black

30

Holy Great Martyr Euphemia

Circa 303 AD
Commemorated — September 16

————

There are two lions in the back section of the book for anyone who would like to add the lions their icon or on the frame of the icon.

Kontakion

Thou didst struggle well in thy contest, and after death dost sanctify us with streams of miracles, O most praised one. Wherefore, we hymn thy holy repose, having recourse to thy divine temple with faith, that we may be delivered from spiritual afflictions, and may draw forth the grace of miracles.

Saint Euphemia was sent into the arena, where lions were sent out to kill her, but instead of attacking her, they licked her wounds.

....

COLOURS

Headcover – Very pale green with gems on bands
Robe – Green
Decoration on Robe – Gold
Cloak – Red

Saint Frideswide
(Frithuswith, Frideswith, Fritheswithe)

Circa +727 AD
Commemorated — October 19

————

Idiomelon – in Tone VIII

Loving Jesus our Saviour with all thy heart and soul, thou didst desire to cleave unto Him alone, O venerable mother; and spurning a royal marriage and all riches on earth, thou didst flee into the wilderness, taking refuge in a cave like the ascetics of old, where in stillness of spirit thou didst hear the voice of God, Who called thee to His banquet on high. Wherefore, O holy Frideswide, thou dwellest with Him forever in paradise, delighting in the ineffable vision of His beloved countenance.

Troparion of the saint – in Tone V

Come, let us solemnly rejoice today, and let us laud the virtues and struggles of the most splendid luminary of the Western lands: Frideswide, great among ascetics, the most praiseworthy instructor of nuns, who watcheth over us from her dwelling-place on high; for the Lord hath truly made her wondrous among His saints. By her supplications may He save our souls.

....

COLOURS

Veil – Dark Blue
Crown – Gold
Schema – Dark Blue / Red Crosses
Trim – Gold
Cloak – Grey / Black
Robe – Orange Ochre
Belt – Brown
Gospel Pages – Venetian Red
Gospel Cover – Gold with Gems
Buildings – Light Grey, Ochre, Green

34

Saint George the Great Martyr

Circa +296 in Nicomedia
Commemorated — April 23

———————

Troparion – in Tone IV

With faith thou didst fight the good fight, O athlete of Christ, didst denounce the ungodliness of the tyrants and didst offer thyself to God as a right acceptable sacrifice. Wherefore, thou hast received a crown of victory, O holy one, and by thy supplications dost bestow the forgiveness of transgressions upon all.

Troparion after the blessing of the loaves – in Tone IV

As a liberator of captives, a helper of the poor, and a physician of the infirm, O champion of kings, victorious great martyr George, entreat Christ God, that our souls be saved.

....

COLOURS

Cloak and stocking – Red
Sleeve – Olive green
Body armour – Deep Blue
Breast band – Violet with gold trim
Waist/hip armour – Indian Red with a touch of deep blue
Skirt – Olive green
Trim above stocking – Gold Black
Horse – Grey and white
Reins and trappings – Red with deep blue and gold
Saddle cloth – Deep blue with touches of burnt sienna
Dragon cave – Dark Brown
Dragon pond – Shades of blue & green
Dragon body – Shades of Green
Dragon wings – Red

Saint Hermione

The Martyr, Unmercenary Physician,
and Daughter of the Apostle Phillip

Circa +117 AD
Commemorated — September 4

––––––––

We know from the Acts of the Apostles that she was a prophetess.
Hermione was a physician and gladly gave of her herself to heal others.
She founded a series of hostels where the sick and dying were given
loving care and treatment and she also became widely acclaimed as a
worker of miraculous healings.

Acts 21:8-9 (KJV)

'On the next day we who were Paul's companions departed and came to
Caesarea, and entered the house of Philip the evangelist, who was one of
the seven, and stayed with him. Now this man had four virgin daughters
who prophesied.'

. . . .

COLOURS

Head Cover – Plum
Garment Medicine – Ultramarine Violet or Brilliant Violet
Box – Plum with Gold highlights
Hair – Dark Brown with highlights

38

Saint Ita of Abbess of Killeedy

(Foster Mother of Saints)

Circa 480 – 570
Commemorated — January 15

————

At Vespers On 'Lord, I have cried...'

Christ God hath bestowed thee upon Ireland as a treasure beyond all reckoning; for, having struggled there for the virtues, O most glorious Ita, thou drivest away hordes of the demons by thine mighty intercession. Wherefore, with joy we bless thee and celebrate thy memory today.

Matins, Ode III – Sessional hymn

The venerable Ita, the adornment of Erin, prayeth ever for the souls of the Irish people; for, having nurtured saints in piety and the true Faith, she now abideth with the angelic hosts in paradise, where she sendeth up unceasing supplications in behalf of those who honour her holy memory.

....

COLOURS

Head Cover – Yellow and Cream/White highlights
Cloak – Indian Red with highlights of Napthol Red Light
Under Garment – Same as Head Cover or a light apricot tone
Schema – Carbon Black with highlights
Belt – Black
Church – Yellow Oxide mix with Raw Siena and Warm White

SAINT ITA

FOSTER MOTHER

OF SAINTS

Saint Juliana
The Merciful of Lazarevo

Circa 1530 – 1604
Commemorated — January 2

———

Troparion

By your righteous deeds you revealed to the world an image of the perfect servant of the Lord. By your fasting, vigil and prayers, you were inspired in your evangelical life, feeding the hungry and caring for the poor, nursing the sick and strengthening the weak. Now you stand at the right hand of the Master, Christ, O holy Juliana, interceding for our souls.

....

COLOURS

Hat – Indian Red Oxide, Napthol Red Light with gems
Veil – Warm White, touch of Napthol Red Light
Cloak – Indian Red Oxide, Napthol Red Light
Design on Cloak – Yellow or Gold
Fur on Cloak and Hat – Brownish
Under Garment – Terre Verte, Chrome Oxide Green, Bohemian Green
Cloth – Warm White

42

Saint Killian
(Cillian, Cilian or Kilian)

Circa 689 AD
Commemorated — July 8

———

Saint Kilian is a the patron saint for sufferers of rheumatism, gout, eye disease, wine growers and shepherds.

Troparion – in Tone IV

An Irishman, you went with eleven companions, To bring the Gospel to pagan peoples. Bishop of Thuringia, you convinced The Duke to break his illegitimate union His Illicit wife caused you to be killed. Saint Kilian, pray to God to save our souls.

. . . .

COLOURS

Hood and schema – Dark Green
Cloak – Deep Red
Garment – Honey yellow
Belt – Black
Background – Green Oxide

ІС ХС
НІ КА

44

Saint Lydia
New Martyr of Russia

Circa 1901 – 1928
Commemorated — July 20

———

Toparion

By the grace of thy meekness, a persecutor's soul was swiftly changed to thy guardian and fellow Martyr in Christ, and through thee attained to God, O righteous Lydia; for that great strength of love in thee overcame the power of darkness and brought thee through the tempest. O Saint of God, take us with thee, as thou didst Cyril and Alexis.

Kontakion – in the Third Tone

Like a quickly spreading fire, the warmth of goodness within thee kindled souls quenched long ago to blaze anew in repentance; and when thou hadst been tormented and life was waning, then the flame of thy great sanctity waxed the brighter, lighting Cyril and Alexis to share thy contest, O Martyr Lydia.

....

COLOURS

Head Covering – Warm White
Coat – Brown Red
Stitching on Coat – Black with Gold trim
Sleeve and Cuffs – Green with Gold trim
Cross – Dark Brown
Gospel book – Indian Red Oxide
Gospel book Cross – Gold
Gospel book Leaves – Gold
Gospel book Edge of pages – Napthol Red Light

Saint Mamas of Caesarea

Circa 275 AD
Commemorated — September 2

––––––––

Saint Basil the Great – Homily 26 – Referring to Saint Mamas

'Keep the holy martyr in remembrance, you who have beheld him in a vision; you who have gathered in this place, having him as your helper; you who have called on his name, and have been granted success in your undertakings; you who were once in error and have been guided by him into life; you who have been healed of your infirmities; you whose children, though dead, have been returned to life; you whose lives have been prolonged. Let all of us who have assembled here send up praise to the martyr'

....

COLOURS

Cloak – Red / Vermilion
Full Garment – Celadon or Chromium Oxide Green
Boots – Green and Gold
Socks – Red
Lamb – Grey and White
Background terrain – Sap Green and Yellow Ochre
Background above terrain – Prussian Blue
Lion – Gold Oxide, Yellow Oxide, Raw Sienna

48

Saint Mamas of Caesarea
(with frame)

Circa 275 AD
Commemorated — September 2

————

I was asked to make a pattern of Saint Mamas based on a 16th century icon in Cyprus. The client very kindly offered to permit me to add the pattern to this book. The pattern was made for wood carving, so there may be features that an iconographer may not want to use in creating an icon but I am sure that many will agree that it is a valuable pattern to have in this volume.

Troparion in Tone IV – Holy Martyr Mamas

In his suffering, O Lord, Thy martyr Mamas received an imperishable crown from Thee our God; for, possessed of Thy might, he set at nought the tormenters and crushed the feeble audacity of the demons. By his supplications save Thou our souls.

....

COLOURS

Cloak – Red / Vermilion
Full Garment – Celadon or Chromium Oxide Green
Boots – Green and Gold
Socks – Red
Lamb – Grey and White
Background terrain – Sap Green and Yellow Ochre
Background above terrain – Prussian Blue
Lion – Gold Oxide, Yellow Oxide, Raw Sienna

Saint Nicholas

Archbishop of Myra in Lycia (Demre in Turkey)

Circa 270 – 343
Commemorated — December 6

Kontakion

In Myra thou wast shown to be a performer of the sacred mysteries, O holy one, for, fulfilling the Gospel of Christ, thou didst lay down thy life for thy people, O venerable one, and didst save the innocent from death. Wherefore, thou hast been sanctified as a great initiate of the grace of God.

At the ordination of Nicholas to presbyter, the Bishop remarked:

'I see, brethren, a new sun rising above the earth and manifesting in himself a gracious consolation for the afflicted. Blessed is the flock that will be worthy to have him as its pastor, because this one will shepherd well the souls of those who have gone astray, will nourish them on the pasturage of piety, and will be a merciful helper in misfortune and tribulation.'

At Nicholas's consecration as Bishop:

'Brethren, receive your shepherd whom the Holy Spirit himself anointed and to whom he entrusted the care of your souls. He was not appointed by an assembly of men but by God himself. Now we have the one that we desired, and have found and accepted the one we sought. Under his rule and instruction we will not lack the hope that we will stand before God in the day of his appearing and revelation.'

COLOURS

Background – Gold Leaf or Neutral Golden Background Paint
Robe – Indian Red Oxide with highlights of Napthol Red
Stole – Light Cream (rather than White
Stole Stiching – Gold
Cross Main – Deep Red or Black
Cross inner – Gold or Red
Neckline – Gold, with gems

Righteous Noah

Commemorated — December 13

Matthew 24:36-39 (KJV)

But of that day and hour knoweth no man, no, not the angels of heaven, but my Father only. But as the days of Noah were, so shall also the coming of the Son of man be. For as in the days that were before the flood they were eating and drinking, marrying and giving in marriage, until the day that Noe entered into the ark, And knew not until the flood came, and took them all away; so shall also the coming of the Son of man be.

....

COLOURS

Background – Dark Indigo
Hair – Grey highlights in white
Cloak – Cobalt Blue Hue/Antique Green/Aqua
Top Garment – Payne's Grey mixed with Naphol Light Red and White
Ark – Burnt Sienna

54

Saint Oda of Brabant
(The Blind Princess of Scotland)

Circa 680 – 726
Commemorated — November 28

————

Saint Oda, the princess of Scotland was born blind. Prayers were constantly offered up for her healing. Her parents heard of the many healings taking place in Liege, Belgium, at the grave of Saint Lambert: they immediately made plans to take their daughter to Liege.

Oda was healed during the family's visit to Belgium and she made a vow to God, promising to dedicate her life to Him from that day forth. Her father however, chose a husband for her. Distressed, Oda took a maid servant and secretly fled from her home. They travelled the Netherlands and found a remote area where they hoped to be hidden. After a time the local people, seeing a large gathering of birds flocking in a group of trees, discovered the two ascetics. People from all the surrounding areas came in a steady stream to ask for prayer, advice and healing.

The night Saint Oda died, a pillar light was seen rising from her hut toward the heavens. The locals, thinking that the saint's hut was on fire, raced to assist her but on arrival they found that there was no fire; their dear saint had reposed. The place where they buried her drew countless believers over the years and God granted many miracles of healing and consolation to the faithful.

....

COLOURS

Head Covering – Storm Blue or Pthalo Blue or Prussian Blue
Cloak – Indian Red Oxide or Madder Red, with Napthol Red
Garment – Storm Blue or Prussian Blue
Bird – Black and White
Belt – Black or brown
Cross – Wood colour
Candle – Yellow Ochre

Saint Paul of Thebes

Circa 227 – 341 AD
Commemorated — January 15

————

Kontakion of the Venerable Paul – Tone III, 'Today the Virgin'

Assembling today let us praise in hymns the never-failing lamp of the noetic Sun; for thou didst shine forth upon those in the darkness of ignorance, leading all to the divine heights, O venerable Paul, adornment of the Thebans, steadfast foundation of the fathers and the venerable.

....

COLOURS

Background – Golden or Deep Blue
Hat and Robe – Cadmium Orange and Gold Oxide
Rocks – Raw Sienna and Warm White
Ground – Sandy colour
Lions – Gold Oxide and Raw Sienna

Saint Sampson the Hospitable

Circa June 27, 598
Commemorated — June 27

―――――――

After having lived many years in prayer and compassion, Saint Sampson fell asleep in the Lord in peace at an advanced age. On his feast day, the doctors in Constantinople would gather in procession, since they honoured him as their patron. In later years, a host of miracles and healings occurred in the hospice through the silent mediation of the Saint or after he made an appearance.

Kontakion

Rejoicing with psalms and hymns, O divinely wise and venerable Sampson, and hastening to your divine shrine, as to that of an excellent physician and a right acceptable intercessor we glorify Christ Who bestows upon you such grace of healing.

....

COLOURS

Cloak – Brown
Garment – Red Earth
Belt – Brown tones
Ointment jar – Warm White with touches of Brown

Saint Spyridon the Wonderworker

Bishop of Trymithous

Circa 270 – 348
Commemorated — December 12

———————

Kontakion

You were shown forth as a champion of the first Council and a wonderworker, O Spyridon, our God-bearing father. You spoke to one dead in the grave, and changed a serpent into gold. And, whilst chanting your holy prayers, you had angels ministering with you, O most sacred one. Glory to Him Who glorified you; glory to Him Who crowned you; Glory to Him that works healings for all through you!

Kontakion

Wounded with love for Christ, and giving wings to your mind given wings by the radiance of the Spirit, you put the practice of theory into deeds, becoming a sacred altar, O Chosen by God, and praying for the divine illumination of all.

....

COLOURS

Phelonion top – Norwegian Orange/ Napthol Crimson/ Cadmium Orange
Phelonion Lining top – Napthol Crimson
Sticharion – Eggshell White / Bavarian Green Earth / Antique Green
Sticharion Lining – Alizarine Crimson dark/ Napthol Crimson & Red
Epimanikia cuffs – Same as Phelonian
Stole with Crosses – Eggshell White/ Bavarian Green Earth
Straw Mitre Hat – Deep straw colours
Cushion – Napthol Red Lights
Throne – Wood tones

Saint Stylianos (Stylian)

Protector of Children

Circa 6th – 7th Century
Commemorated — November 26

————

Through his prayers many miracles have been experienced, right up
to the present day. Saint Stylianos is asked to intercede for whose are
ill or distressed, childless couples who desire to have a child and he is
also known as a protector of orphans.

Troparion – in Tone IV

As a worker of God-given wonders, and a protector of the youth
and infants, O Stylianos, our Father and healer of Christ, grant
children to barren mothers, and ever cover newborn babes, for to
you was richly granted grace from God, as you struggled for Him in
asceticism as an angel.

Pour forth grace from your holy icon, through the covering of the
Spirit, O father, and nourish and gladden newborns and infants.

· ·

COLOURS

Cloak – Norwegian Orange
Robe – Yellow Oxide
Schema – Storm Blue (Dark Blue) / Touch of black
Babe's Wrapping – Nimbus Grey / Warm White
Small patterns on fabric – Use soft colours – blues, pinks, green, etc.

BUT JESUS SAID, ALLOW THE LITTLE CHILDREN AND

FORBID THEM NOT, TO COME UNTO ME,

FOR SUCH IS THE KINGDOM OF HEAVEN. MATTHEW 19:1

Holy Martyrs Timothy & Maura

Circa 286
Commemorated — May 3

———

Troparion

In their sufferings, O Lord, Thy martyrs received imperishable crowns
from Thee, our God; for, possessed of Thy might, they set at nought
the tyrants and crushed the feeble audacity of the demons. By their
supplications save Thou our souls.

Kontakion

Having endured multifarious wounds and received crowns from God,
pray ye to the Lord in behalf of us who celebrate your most sacred
memory, O Timothy all-great and all-glorious Maura, that He grant
peace to our city and people; for He is the confirmation of the faithful.

Prayer – Hymn from St. Nikolai Velimirovich

O Saints Timothy and Maura pray to God for Christian marriages,
that spouses may be strong in love and rejoice in suffering together,
encouraging each other daily to grow in Christ.

....

COLOURS

Timothy Robe – Moss Green or Bavarian Green
Timothy Cloak – Norwegian Orange or Translucent Orange-Red
Timothy Cuff – Yellow Ochre
Maura Head Cover – Warm White or Lead White with a touch of colour
Maura Under Robe – Celadon or light Blue Azarite
Maura Cuffs – Y ellow Ochre
Maura Cloak – Indian Red Oxide or Madder Lake Bordeaux Red

Saint Xenia of Kalamata

291 AD
Commemorated — May 3

———

Saint Xenia was born in 291 AD and as she grew up, she grew in faith and love of God. The Magistrate of Kalamata (a non-believer) saw Xenia and desired to marry her; but she rejected his proposal. In anger he had her brought before him and when all his flattery and promises failed to make her deny Christ, he had her imprisoned and tortured. After months of persecution she refused to deny her faith in God, so she was condemned to death. The Christians, who loved and respected Xenia, took her body and arranged a Christian burial.

Soon after her death, and right up to this very day, miracles have been reported through the intercession of Saint Xenia of Kalamata. People have been healed of incurable diseases, heart disease, mental illnesses, nervous disorders, boils, ulcers and paralysis.

From pravoslabvie.ru:
The icon of St Xenia still adorns the Greek Archdiocese Annunciation Church in New York City and has for forty years been the site of miracles, and miracles in this twentieth century have been hard to come by.

....

COLOURS

Background – Gold
Hair – Light brown
Cloak – Venetian Red
Under Garment – Pthalo Green and Antique Green
Cross – Raw Sienna with Dark Brown detail

Anzer Cross

Elevation of the Cross – September 14

Hymn sung many times during the Services of the feast of the Elevation of the Holy Cross: Before Thy Cross we bow down bow down in worship, O Master, and Thy holy Resurrection we glorify!

This Feast is an to celebrate the full significance of the victory of the Cross over the powers of the world, and the triumph of the wisdom of God through the Cross over the wisdom of this world.

Veneration of the Holy Cross – 3rd Sunday of Great Lent

Hymn sung many times during the Services of the feast of the Veneration of the Holy Cross: Before Thy Cross we bow down bow down in worship, O Master, and Thy holy Resurrection we glorify!

O Lord, save Your people and bless Your inheritance; grant victory to the faithful over their adversaries. And protect Your commonwealth, by the power of Your Cross.

....

This pattern can be used on a cut-out cross board or on a flat board with borders, anywhere from 1" (about (3cms) to 3" (7.62cms) wide.

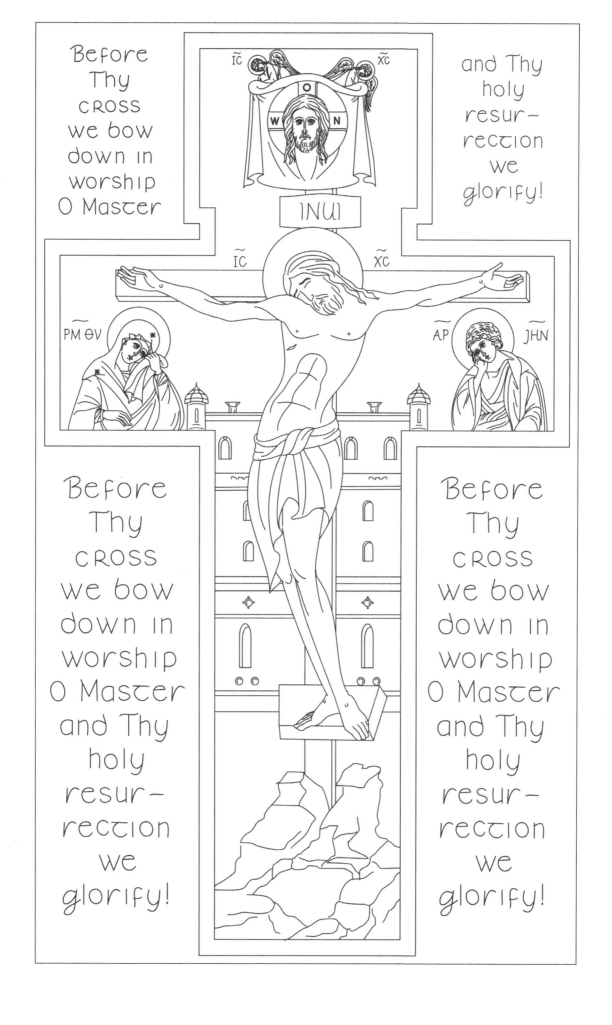

Before Thy cross we bow down in worship O Master

and Thy holy resurrection we glorify!

Before Thy cross we bow down in worship O Master and Thy holy resurrection we glorify!

Before Thy cross we bow down in worship O Master and Thy holy resurrection we glorify!

70

Fabric – Background Patterns

Most of the following patterns could be used as a fabric design but could also, very successfully, be used as a background pattern.

Background patterns can be raised with gold leaf laid on over top of the pattern or can be painted over with the background colour. Alternatively, a background can be imprinted on top of gold leaf.

The patterns that have uneven borders, are made like that so that in a large icon, the pattern can be spliced together for the larger space.

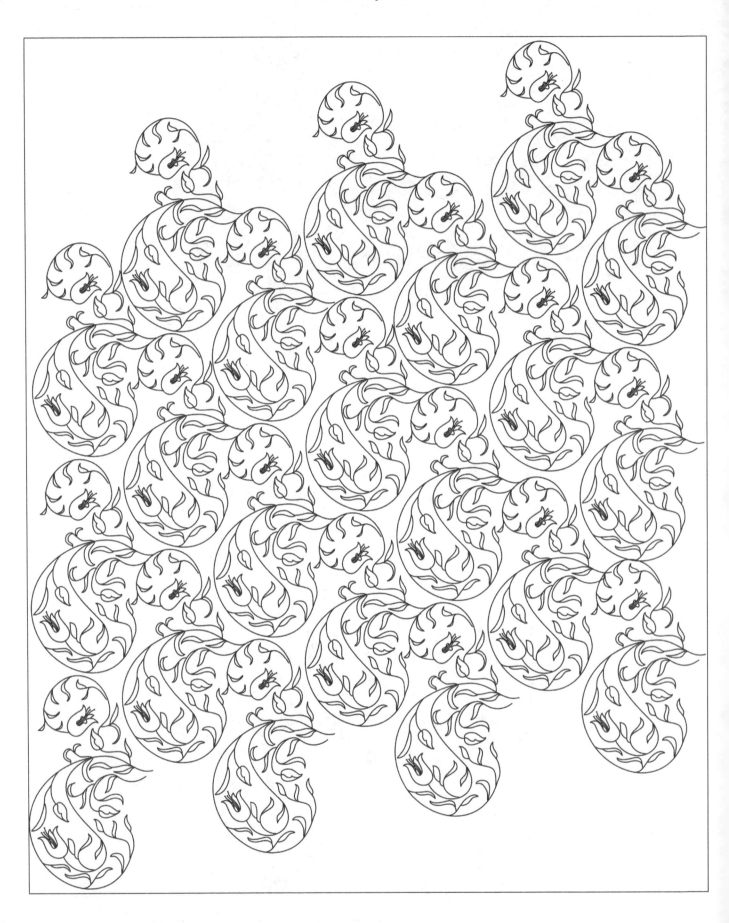

Borders

——————

Icons very often don't have patterned borders but there are times
when they are used, particularly when the icon is of high value or the
iconographer would like to make it a bit more decorative because the icon
is to be placed in a church.

If one were to produce say, two or three icons as a set, it would be nice to
have all three with the same border design.

One can feel free to use colours on these borders.

84

Border — **Angel** (Ethiopian Style)

Border — **Ropely** (Ethiopian Style)

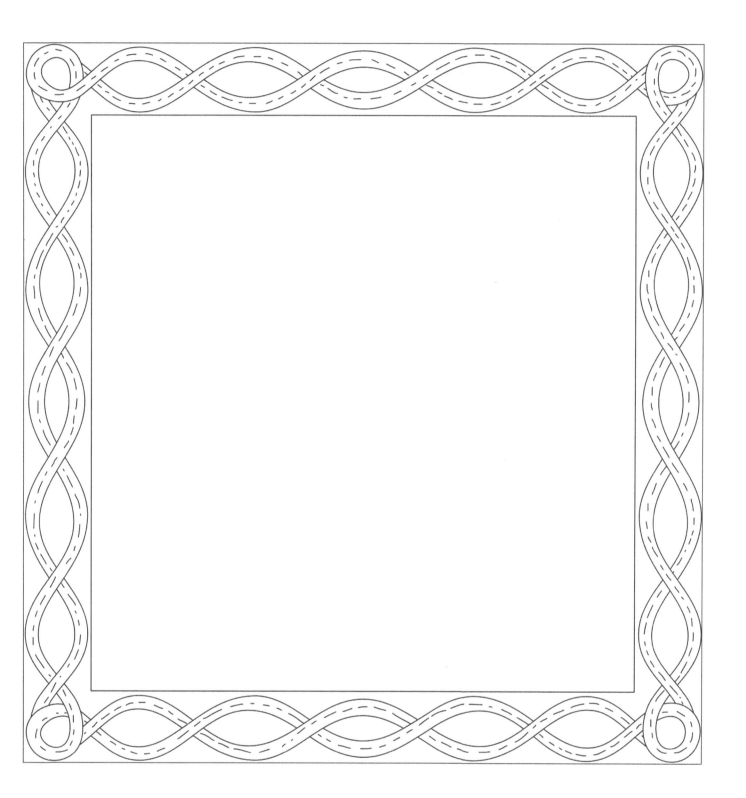

Border — **Star** (Ethiopian Style)

Halos

When the icon is of the Theotokos and the Christ Child, the two halos will match, although the one for the Christ Child will not contain as much detail decoration.

These patterns can be imprinted on gold leaf or for raised designs that will be covered with gold leaf, egg tempera or paint.

They can also be used for metal decoration.

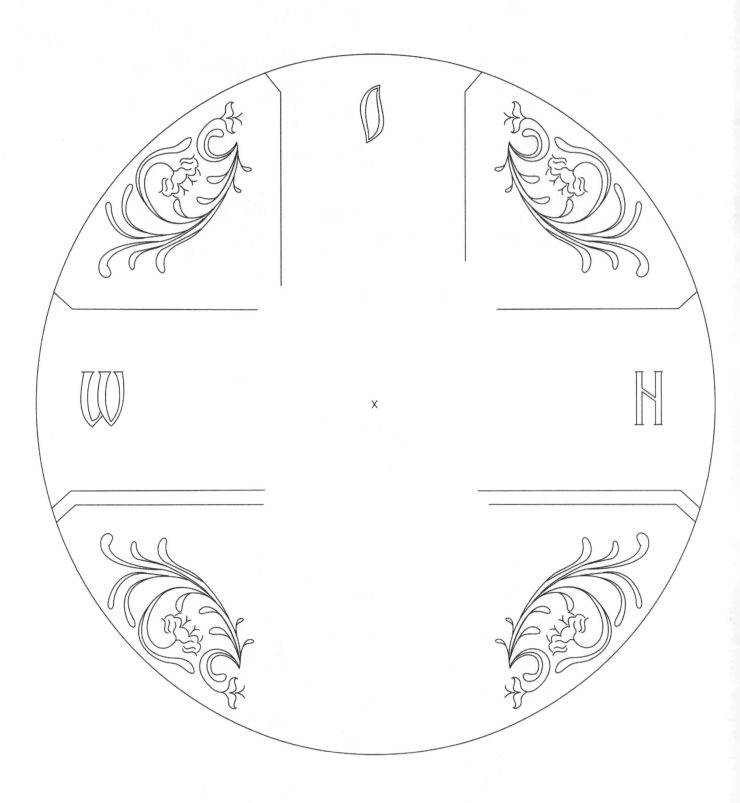

Lettering

———

Included are 4 different styles of lettering which could be used for names on your icons: Almaznyye, Danica, Evgenia and Theodore.

Script — **Almaznyye**

Script — **Danica**
(Morning Star)

Script — **Evgenia**

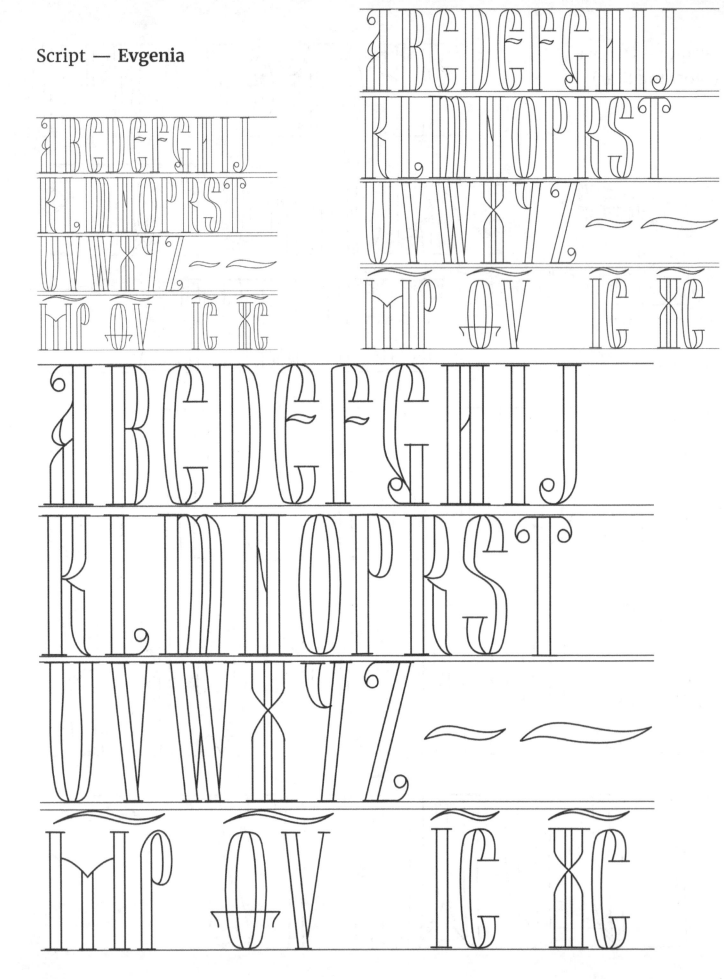

Script — Theodore

ABCDEFGHIJ
KLMNOPQRS
TUVWXYZ
HP OY IC XC

ABCDEFGHIJ
KLMNOPQRS
TUVWXYZ
HP OY IC XC

A Prayer for New Icons Donated to the Church

Glory be to the Father, to the Son and to the Holy Spirit.

O Lord, God of the whole incorporeal and perceptible creation, the Maker of the heavenly hosts, the earthly beings and all that is under the earth, You have filled Your Church with the likeness of the first-born who are written in Your Heavenly Church and who minister to You with Your Holy Spirit. Grant, O Lord God, that Your powerful and omnipotent right hand may protect, bless and sanctify this icon for the adoration of Your Most Honored Name. May all those who call upon You in true faith and ask of Your compassion with a pure heart, receive their good requests and present to You first-fruits and oblations for obtaining health and healing and for attaining salvation of their souls. We beseech You and make supplication to You to accomplish Your command and fulfill the promise of Your Most Holy Spirit so that the Gospel precept may dwell, operate, perfect and be diligent regarding every deed or word that is done or said in the name of this icon. We ask this favor by Your loving-kindness, the mercies and the philanthropy of Your Only-begotten Son, our Lord God and Savior Jesus Christ, with Whom befit You praise, honor and dominion with Your Holy Spirit, now, always and forever.

Chanter: Amen.
Priest: O Lord our God, by the prayers of Your Mother and of all Your saints, martyrs, apostles and Saint (Name).

Here he anoints the icon with oil, not chrism, saying:
In the Name of the Father +.
Chanter: Amen.
And of the Son +.
Chanter: Amen.
And of the Holy Spirit + for life eternal.
Chanter: Amen.

The Blessing of Icons

After the trisagian prayers...

Priest: Your saints we venerate as being in Your Image O Lord our God, Who created us after Your own Image and Likeness; Who redeems us from our former corruption of the ancient curse through Your man-loving Christ, Who took upon Himself the form of a servant and became man; Who having taken upon Himself our likeness remade Your Saints of the first dispensation, and through Whom also we are refashioned in the Image of Your pure blessedness; and Likeness, and we adore and glorify You as our Creator; Wherefore we pray You, send forth Your blessing upon this Icon, made in honour and remembrance of Your Saint (Name ...) and with the sprinkling of hallowed water bless and make holy this Icon unto Your glory. And grant that this sanctification will be to all who venerate this Icon of Saint (Name ...), and send up their prayer unto You whilst standing before it. Through the grace and bounties and love of Your Only-Begotten Son, with Whom You are blessed together with Your All-Holy, Good and Life-creating Spirit; both now and ever, and unto ages of ages.

Reader: Amen.
Priest: Peace be unto all
Reader: And unto your spirit
Priest: Bow your heads unto the Lord
Reader: To you, O Lord

The Priest shall bow his head and says this prayer:
For You are He that blesses and sanctifies all things, O Christ our God, and to You we send up glory, together with Your Father Who is without beginning, and Your Most-holy, Good and Life-creating Spirit, now and ever and unto ages of ages. Amen.

Priest: Sprinkling (in the form of the cross) the Icon with Holy Water the priest says: Hallowed and blessed is this Icon of Saint (Name ...) by the Grace of the Holy Spirit, through the sprinkling of Holy Water: in the Name of the Father (+), and of the Son (+) and of the Holy Spirit: (+), Amen.

And having sprinkled it, the Priest shall cense it and venerate and kiss it. The People shall sing the Troparion of the Saint or event depicted by the icon, and the Priest shall pronounce the Dismissal mentioning the Feast or Saint.

Order for the Blessing & Sanctification of Icons

After the trisagian prayers... Let us pray to the Lord. Lord have mercy.

O Lord Almighty, God of our Fathers, glorified and worshiped in the Holy Trinity, Whom neither mind is able to comprehend nor word able to express, Whom no one among men has ever seen, as we have learned from the Holy Scriptures, thus we believe and thus we confess You, God the Father without beginning, and Your Son, one in essence, co-enthroned with Your Spirit. In the Old Law You revealed Yourself to Your Patriarch Abraham in the image of the three Angels, and in the latter days after the Incarnation of the Only-begotten Son of God, our Lord Jesus Christ, from the Ever-virgin Mary, in the Baptism by John in the Jordan, in the truly- bright Transfiguration on Tabor, in the most-glorious Ascension on Olivet, You showed us the image of the Most-holy Trinity; You instructed us also to honour the wonderworking Image Not- Made-By-Hands of our Lord Jesus Christ depicted on the towel and sent to Abgar, the Prince of Edessa, which healed him and many others sick with the wounds of sickness; You did not reject, but accepted also the images and likeness of Your holy Saints. Look down now, also, on this (these) Icon(s) which Your servants have fashioned in honour and glory of You, (One in Trinity, the Holy and Glorious God,) (and Your Only-begotten Son, our Lord Jesus Christ,) (and Your most-pure and truly-blessed Mother, our Sovereign Lady, the Most-holy Theotokos and Ever- virgin Mary,) and in memory of Your Saint(s) [NAMES],) and bless it (them) and sanctify it (them) and grant it (them) healing power, that it (they) may drive away every snare of the devil, that it (they) may cause the prayers of all diligently praying before it (them) to be heard, that they may draw down Your mercy and love for mankind, and that they may receive Grace. For You are our sanctification, and to You we send up glory, to the Father, and to the Son, and to the Holy Spirit, now and ever and unto ages of ages. Amen.

Peace be unto all.
And to your spirit.
Bow your heads to the Lord. To You, O Lord.

The Priest shall bow his head and says this prayer:

O eternal, invisible and incomprehensible Lord, Who in ancient times, in the Old Law, commanded that in the Tent of the Testimony and Temple of Solomon there be made likenesses of the cherubim of wood, gold and embroidery, and Who now accepts images not only in remembrance of Your saving benefactions and divine manifestations to the Human race, made in honour and glory of Your most-holy Name, but also do not reject those fashioned in remembrance of and in imitation of Your holy Saints, attend to our humble prayer: Bless this (these) Icon(s) and sanctify it (them), and grant it (them) grace and power to drive out demons and to heal all infirmities:

For You are He that blesses and sanctifies all things, O Christ our God, and to You we send up glory, together with Your Father Who is without beginning, and Your Most-holy, Good and Life-creating Spirit, now and ever and unto ages of ages. Amen.

The Priest shall sprinkle the icon(s) with Holy Water, saying:

This icon is (these icons are) sanctified by the grace of the All-holy Spirit, through the sprinkling of this holy water: In the Name of the Father, and of the Son, and of the Holy Spirit. Amen (Thrice).

And having sprinkled it, the Priest shall cense it and venerate and kiss it. The People shall sing the Troparion of the Saint or event depicted by the icon, and the Priest shall pronounce the Dismissal mentioning the Feast or Saint.

A Prayer for Consecrating an Iconographer

———

Glory to the Father and of the Son and of the Holy Spirit, both now and ever, and unto ages of ages. Amen.

O Thou Who so admirably imprinted Thy features on the cloth sent to King Abgar of Edessa, and so wonderfully inspired Luke the Evangelist, enlighten my soul and that of Thy servant (Name). Guide his/her hand that he/she may reproduce Thy features, those of the Holy Virgin and of all Thy saints, for the glory and peace of Thy Holy Church. Spare him/her from temptations and diabolical imaginations through the intercession of Thy most Holy Mother, Saint Luke, and all the Saints.

In the name of the Father and of the Son and of the Holy Spirit, both now and ever and unto ages of ages. Amen.

Iconographer's Prayer

"O Divine Lord of all that exists, You illumined the Apostle and Evangelist Luke with Your Most Holy Spirit, thereby enabling him to represent Your most Holy Mother, the one who held You in her arms and said: 'the Grace of Him Who has been born of me is spread throughout the world.'"

Enlighten and direct our souls, our hearts and our spirits. Guide the hands of your unworthy servant, so that we may worthily and perfectly portray your icon, that of Your Holy Mother and of all the saints, for the glory and adornment of Your Holy Church. Forgive our sins and the sins of those who will venerate these icons, and who, standing devoutly before them, give homage those they represent. Protect them from all evil and instruct them with good counsel. This we ask through the prayers of the Most Holy Theotokos, the Apostle Luke, and all the saints, now and ever and unto ages of ages. Amen.

Index — Date of Commemoration

JANUARY	Saint Juliana	January 2
	Saint Ita of Abbess of Killeedy	January 15
	Saint Paul of Thebes	January 15
	Saint Dwynwen	January 25
FEBRUARY	Saint Apollonia	February 9
APRIL	Saint George the Great Martyr	April 23
	Saint Argyre	April 30
MAY	Saint Xenia of Kalamata	May 3
	Saints Timothy & Maura	May 3
	Saint Ephraim of Nea Makri	May 5
JUNE	Saint Columba	June 6
	Saint Agrippina of Rome	June 23
	Saint David of Thessalonica	June 26
	Saint Sampson the Hospitable	June 27
JULY	Saint Aidan	July 4
	Saint Killian	July 8
	Saint Lydia	July 20
AUGUST	Saint Andrew	August 31
SEPTEMBER	Saint Mamas of Caesarea (1)	September 2
	Saint Mamas of Caesarea (2)	Septmeber 2
	Saint Hermione	September 4
	Saint Euphemia	September 16
OCTOBER	Saint Frideswide	October 19
NOVEMBER	Archangel Michael	November 8
	Saint Cecilia	November 22
	Saint Stylianos (Stylian)	November 26
	Saint Oda of Brabant	November 28
DECEMBER	Saint Nicholas	December 6
	Saint Spyridon	December 12
	Righteous Noah	December 13

Index — Name of Saint

Archangel Michael	November 8
Saint Agrippina of Rome	June 23
Saint Aidan	July 4
Saint Andrew	August 31
Saint Apollonia	February 9
Saint Argyre	April 30
Saint Cecilia	November 22
Saint Columba	June 6
Saint David of Thessalonica	June 26
Saint Dwynwen	January 25
Saint Ephraim of Nea Makri	May 5
Saint Euphemia	September 16
Saint Frideswide	October 19
Saint George the Great Martyr	April 23
Saint Hermione	September 4
Saint Ita of Abbess of Killeedy	January 15
Saint Juliana	January 2
Saint Killian	July 8
Saint Lydia	July 20
Saint Mamas of Caesarea (1)	September 2
Saint Mamas of Caesarea (2)	September 2
Saint Nicholas	December 6
Righteous Noah	December 13
Saint Oda of Brabant	November 28
Saint Paul of Thebes	January 15
Saint Sampson the Hospitable	June 27
Saint Spyridon	December 12
Saint Stylianos (Stylian)	November 26
Saints Timothy & Maura	May 3
Saint Xenia of Kalamata	May 3

About the Author

RB Cass has been drawing icon patterns for over 20 years. Over this period of time she has accumulated a diverse collection which includes icon patterns as well as carving patterns and colouring books.

I would love to see photographs of your icons, painted using these patterns, or answer any questions you may have. With your permission, we would love to share your images online.

If you have enjoyed this book please consider leaving a review, a massive amount of time was spent creating the book, feedback is always welcome.

email: **patternmakers@yahoo.com**

Made in United States
Cleveland, OH
02 June 2025

17424896R00066